western
australia

Steve Parish™

PUBLISHING

Previous page: Wildflowers in Mt Augustus National Park.

Above: The southern coast of Western Australia is noted for its magnificent beaches.

Introduction

There is a journey through Western Australia which every nature lover should make at least once in a lifetime. This journey has its start in the Kimberley, the remote northern part of the State, in June and July, when dry winter conditions allow access to rugged ranges, monsoon woodlands and plains. The adventure continues with a leisurely drive down the coast, past Broome and along Eighty Mile Beach, so that early August is spent in the Pilbara amidst magnificent scenery and fascinating wildlife. Then the explorer should move south in stages, with stopovers at attractions ranging from fields of wildflowers to friendly wild dolphins and the fantastic Pinnacles of Nambung National Park. At the end of this journey are the delights of the State capital, Perth and the nearby port of Fremantle, with a voyage to Rottnest Island as the crowning touch.

Another wonderful expedition takes the traveller through the green south-west of the State, with its tall Karri trees, vineyards, orchards and scenic coastline. This route turns eastwards from Cape Leeuwin and eventually allows the wanderer to revel in the splendour of some of the finest unspoiled coastline remaining in the world today.

The historically-minded should follow the long, straight highway that runs east from Perth to the Goldfields area, where, since the late nineteenth century, fortunes have been made and lost. This arid country, with its picturesque relics of the mining days, is best tackled during the cooler months of the year.

It's a huge State, and I for one never grow tired of exploring its vastness and marvelling at the beauty of the panoramas which confront me at every turn of the road. The images in this book pay tribute to some of the aspects of Western Australia I love best.

Steve Parish

Perth, the riverside city

The Swan River winds through the heart of Perth, bordered by green parks and cycling tracks, dividing the glittering towers of the city's business heart from the prosperous suburbs that grace its southern bank. It provides Western Australia's capital with a focus, a playground and a vista that changes from a placid navy-blue to a ruffled silver-grey as weather fronts roll in from the Indian Ocean to the west.

Perth is divided by more than 2000 kilometres from the nearest State capital. Its population of about 2 million people treasures the relaxed Perth lifestyle. While many of Perth's people journey far from the city on the Swan River, the majority of them return to make their homes in this spacious, gracious city with its magnificent Mediterranean climate and hospitable atmosphere.

Perth city centre, viewed across the Swan River.

A view across the Swan River and Point Currie to Kings Park, Mill Point, the Narrows Bridge, Perth Water and the Perth central business district.

The Swan Bells in Barrack Square comprise the 12 bells of St Martin-in-the-Fields, London, a bicentennial gift to WA, and 6 new bells, making one of the world's largest sets of change-ringing bells.

Above: The Narrows Bridge leads to Perth's central business district.

Following pages: Beyond Perth Water rises the elegant city skyline.

Previous pages: The city, surrounded by parks, is a people-friendly centre.

Above: Forrest House, a reconstruction of the residence of Alexander Forrest, among the city high-rise.

The heart of the city

The Hay Street Mall entrance to London Court.

Hay Street Mall.

In Perth, the historical and the modern blend in charming and orderly fashion. Heritage buildings have been lovingly restored and provide fascinating accents amongst the big-city towers which have appeared following Western Australia's leap in prosperity over the past few decades. Modernisation has been well thought out. Hay Street, in the heart of Perth, was once a narrow thoroughfare, cluttered with motor vehicles, but is now a busy and popular mall. London Court, which leads from the mall to St Georges Terrace, is a mock-Tudor landmark. It was opened in 1937 and its boutiques attract interested shoppers.

The city centre and Swan River can be viewed from Kings Park's many vantage points.

Kings Park

Kings Park has extensive gardens of native wildflowers and feature displays of other countries' flora.

The wonderful eucalypt and banksia woodlands and magnificent wildflower gardens of Kings Park form a 400-hectare oasis on the slopes and summit of Mt Eliza, overlooking the Swan River and Perth city centre. The park features an excellent restaurant and cafe and a number of picnicking and barbecue areas. The statue of Lord Forrest of Bunbury stands near the park's two War Memorials: other attractions are the trunk of a giant Karri tree, the DNA Tower and the Pioneer Womens Memorial Fountain.

Wildflower heaven

The area on Mt Eliza now occupied by Kings Park was called by the Aboriginal Nyoongah people *Mooro Katta*, an all-sit-down-place, or friendly ground.

Since the park's formal establishment in 1895, it has survived attempts to allocate land for other uses and defied the ravages of bushfires. Dedicated volunteers and hard-working staff have successfully implemented ambitious plans which include a marvellous Botanic Garden, botanical research facilities, and the popular Wildflower Festival which sees thousands visit the park each September. As the picture at left shows, this is truly a wild place in the heart of a city.

Wildflowers carpet the ground in Kings Park.

Mallee blossoms and buds.

Scarlet Bottlebrush.

Morning Iris.

Orange Banksia.

18

Mangles' Kangaroo Paw.

Cowslip Orchid.

Yellow Flag.

Mottlecah.

Perth's beaches

Opposite: At Scarborough Beach, the tower of Radisson Observation City Hotel overlooks the Indian Ocean.

Above: Cottesloe Beach, a popular family recreation area.

Perth's Mediterranean climate guarantees a warm, dry summer and a delightful, usually rainless spring and autumn. For most months of the year, the glorious beaches that stretch from Port Beach, north of Fremantle, to Burns Beach, at the end of the Mitchell Freeway, are popular places to swim, surf, fish, walk and picnic. In winter, when swimming is less popular, strolling along the beaches in the crisp, cold weather, looking for shells and other flotsam, is a great way to spend weekend hours.

Rottnest Island

Above: The island of Rottnest was explored by Dutch seamen in 1658.

Rottnest is an island 19 kilometres from the coast of Western Australia, 11 kilometres in length and 4.5 kilometres at its widest point. It features five salt lakes which have their own unique wildlife. A short journey by sea and an even briefer one by air, this holiday-makers' paradise is made all the more attractive by a ban on private vehicles, which brings the silent, non-polluting bicycle into its own. For many West Australians, a trip to "Rotto" is the reward for a year's hard work. For visitors to the State, it is a highlight in a journey full of wonderful experiences.

Opposite: The flash of the lighthouse (left) can be seen on the mainland.
Following pages: An aerial view of Fremantle's Success Harbour and Fishing Boat Harbour.

Fremantle

A visitor to the capital of the Golden West gets two cities instead of one. Only 19 kilometres from the centre of Perth, where the Swan River meets the sea, stands the port of Fremantle. The America's Cup competition of 1987 brought new fame and renewed vigour to a place whose historic public and commercial buildings and workaday port facilities had long been taken for granted. Suddenly Fremantle was scrubbed up and rejuvenated for its international media coverage. Once the Cup frenzy was over, many people remembered the city's charm and multicultural vitality. Today, Fremantle is a working port and harbours a large fishing fleet, but it is also home to countless arts and crafts practitioners, has a magnificent Maritime Museum and splendid Arts Centre. Dining and cafe-visiting in Fremantle have outlasted fashion's whim, and the solid limestone and brick cottages that once housed dock workers and factory workers have become sought-after dwellings for those who enjoy the ambience of this fascinating and historic port.

The Round House, built 1830–31, is Fremantle's oldest remaining building, and was the colony's first prison. Bathers Beach, below it, was the site of bay whaling operations.

Western Australia's heritage

The first European towns in Western Australia were Albany and Perth, both established in the late 1820s. Farmers and graziers rapidly extended the boundaries of settlement through the south-western corner of the State and northwards from Perth. Nearly every town had some convenient source of stone, and civic buildings, schools, churches and hostelries quickly graced the streets. These amenities were built to last and today towns such as Bunbury, Busselton, York, Geraldton, Kalgoorlie and Albany proudly display their heritage. Increasingly, visitors from interstate and overseas are exploring the towns of the south-west, the Wheatbelt, Goldfields and Batavia Coast north of Perth, admiring fine examples of nineteenth century architecture which, in many cases, have been restored to their former glory.

Figures on a traffic roundabout contemplate the splendid facade of the Rose Hotel, Bunbury.

The Exchange, one of Kalgoorlie's many hotels, stands near the offices of the famous Goldfields newspaper, the *Kalgoorlie Miner*.

New Norcia was founded in 1846 by the Benedictine order of monks as an Aboriginal mission. Today it is noted for its art gallery and museum.

The ruins of historic Lillimilura Police Station, located within Windjana Gorge National Park.

The remains of the mudbrick post office at Halls Creek, a Kimberley outpost where gold was discovered in 1885.

Albany

Above: A view down Albany's York Street to Princess Royal Harbour. On the right is the Town Hall.

The charming town of Albany, on the south-east coast of Western Australia, was settled by the British in 1826. Its fine harbour meant that it became a thriving whaling port and coaling station. Today, this historic town is an excellent base for exploration of some of Australia's most rugged and spectacular coastal scenery, and for scenic and wildflower tours of Porongurup and the Stirling Range.

Opposite: Albany's old Post Office now houses the Inter-Colonial Museum. In the background is Mt Clarence.

33

Leeuwin–Naturaliste National Park

Leeuwin–Naturaliste National Park, which runs around the coast in a narrow strip from Bunker Bay to Augusta, protects 120 kilometres of scenic grandeur.

The names of the features of this area are steeped in history. In 1622, the Dutch ship *Leeuwin (Lioness)*, gave her name to the cape at the south-west corner of the great southern continent. On 30 May, 1801, the French mariner Nicholas Baudin arrived at Géographe Bay with the ships *Le Géographe* and *Le Naturaliste* on a voyage of scientific discovery.

The shoreline of the park includes rugged cliffs, stark headlands and sheltered, sandy coves. Inland are coastal heathlands, woodlands and forests. In amongst the Jarrah and Marri trees, small patches of Karri, one of the world's tallest trees, can be seen. The Boranup Karri Forest, which was logged extensively in the late nineteenth century, contains regrowth trees up to 60 metres tall. This is the "limestone coast", and the area is famed for its cave systems, with spectacular stalactites and stalagmites.

Regrowth Karri trees and bracken fern, Leeuwin–Naturaliste National Park.

Cape Leeuwin lighthouse stands on the southernmost prominence of Leeuwin–Naturaliste National Park.

Above: Coastal limestone formations, Leeuwin–Naturaliste National Park.   *Following pages:* Sugarloaf Rock, just south of Cape Naturaliste.

Above: A peaceful view of the Warren River, Warren National Park.

Above: Rapids on Beedelup Brook, Beedelup National Park.

Warren, Beedelup and Shannon National Parks

Uncut stands of Karri are a highlight of Warren National Park, near Pemberton, in the tall timber country. Much of this 1400-hectare area can be accessed only on foot by those dedicated to experiencing south-western wilderness. One of the two major routes through this magnificent area is called the Heartbreak Trail, while the other, not noticeably less rugged, has the milder title of the Maidenbush Trail.

Beedelup Brook and Beedelup Falls are attractions of Beedelup National Park, 15 kilometres west of Pemberton. Besides dense Karri forest, this lovely park contains pure stands of Marri, a rough-barked eucalypt whose white flowers provide plentiful nectar for insects and birds.

Shannon National Park is 30 minutes' drive from Pemberton. It covers the basin of the Shannon River and is an ideal place to learn the secrets of Western Australia's famed forests. Look for wildflowers in these parks from October to December.

Opposite: On the road to discoveries in Shannon National Park.

Wave Rock, Hyden

The inland plains to the east and south-east of Perth, first explored by timber-cutters seeking aromatic sandalwood, are now the source of wheat and wool. Isolated outcrops of granite called tors are characteristic of the Wheatbelt, and the little town of Hyden stands near a number of these. The end of one tor, Hyden Rock, forms the remarkable Wave Rock, whose lip hangs 15 metres above the ground.

It has taken around 300 million years of weathering to scour out the area under the overhang. The bands which run up and down the face are caused by dark-coloured algae which grow on streaks of minerals washed down the rock.

Wave Rock is the north wall of Hyden Rock, a huge mass of granite.

The Stirling Range

Above: Springtime in Stirling Range National Park.

The south-west of Western Australia is famous world wide for its wildflowers, which have developed in great variety on comparatively poor soils. Many of these flowers rely on birds, insects and mammals for pollination, so they are rich in nectar. The rugged Stirling Range, which rises to more than 1000 metres above sea level some 80 kilometres north of Albany, and stretches for around 65 kilometres from east to west, is a well known wildflower area. Over 1000 species grow on the various peaks of the range, and at least 60 of these plants are found nowhere else in the world.

Opposite: Wildflowers in Stirling Range National Park.

The spectacular south coast

The south-western corner and southern coast of Western Australia offer scenes of beauty which invite the traveller to stay awhile, explore and forget the stresses of civilisation.

Along the south coast, the edge of the continental shelf (the shallow submerged ledge which normally breaks the force of waves before they reach the coast) lies close inshore. With no undersea ledge to break their force, the surging waves of the Southern Ocean have carved inlets and coves into the coastline and continue to worry away at the massive granite headlands which defy their power.

Getting away from it all in William Bay National Park, a scenic gem between Walpole and Denmark.

47

Above: This treetop walk allows close viewing of a Karri forest canopy.   *Opposite:* Amongst the Tingle tree giants.

Walpole–Nornalup National Park

Waterfalls, massive granite domes and majestic forests are features of this park which surrounds Walpole and Nornalup inlets. A wonderful place for bushwalkers, birdwatchers and photographers, it is also ideal for those who love fishing or just sitting by the sea. Nearby, the impressive Valley of the Giants contains a forest of rare Red Tingle trees, towering above distinctive buttressed roots.

Previous pages: Coastal dunes, Walpole–Nornalup National Park.

Above: Walpole–Nornalup National Park.

Margaret River

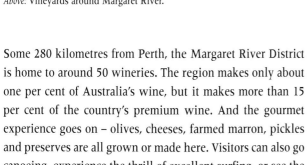

Above: Vineyards around Margaret River.

Above: Margaret River wine lies aging in its barrels.

Some 280 kilometres from Perth, the Margaret River District is home to around 50 wineries. The region makes only about one per cent of Australia's wine, but it makes more than 15 per cent of the country's premium wine. And the gourmet experience goes on – olives, cheeses, farmed marron, pickles and preserves are all grown or made here. Visitors can also go canoeing, experience the thrill of excellent surfing, or see the area's underground crystal caves.

Opposite: Brookfield Estate winery, Margaret River.

Torndirrup National Park

Natural Bridge, Torndirrup National Park.

The dramatic coastal scenery of Torndirrup National Park, only 10 kilometres south of Albany across Princess Royal Harbour, is due to the granite rocks which have been battered by the sea into cliffs such as The Gap, headlands such as Bald Head, and phenomena such as Natural Bridge. Whales swim past these coasts in winter, the fishing is superb and rock climbers and bushwalkers find special joys in the challenging terrain.

Those who fish from the headlands of this awesome coast must guard against the freak giant waves which occasionally surge without warning from a calm sea.

Above: The entrance to Princess Royal Harbour.

Following pages: The Salmon Holes, Torndirrup National Park.

Two Peoples Bay

The nature reserve which extends into the heathland and wooded gullies behind Two Peoples Bay, 20 kilometres east of Albany, is a very important place for nature lovers. Several very rare bird and mammal species, including the endangered Noisy Scrub-bird and Long-footed Potoroo, survive here.

One of the world's remaining great wilderness areas lies around 180 kilometres east of Albany. Fitzgerald River National Park is a haven for wildflower species, including the extraordinary Royal Hakea. It also harbours rare mammals, and is classed as a World Biosphere Reserve.

Two Peoples Bay, named to commemorate peaceful contact between French and English ships on this coast two centuries ago.

Cape Le Grand National Park, near the port of Esperance.

An unspoiled beach in Fitzgerald River National Park.

Eucla National Park

The sand dunes, heathlands and mallee which comprise Eucla National Park are near the border dividing Western Australia from South Australia. The lover of nature, who appreciates the impressive sand dunes, with their subtle tints and sensuous shapes, will find the view of the spectacular sea cliffs which border the Great Australian Bight worth the lack of normal tourist amenities. The traveller who wishes to experience Australia's ancient landscapes, or observe first-hand the ever-changing face of Nature, will find Eucla National Park, where shifting sands slowly but surely engulf anything in their path, both beautiful and inspiring.

Footsteps across the sand dunes at Eucla.

Above: Dry woodlands border the salt lakes in the south-east of the State.

Above: The Nullarbor, the flat coastal plain north of the Great Australian Bight, becomes bright with flowers after rainfall.

The Nullarbor

A number of reserves protect the flora and fauna of Western Australia's arid south-eastern corner. Nature reserves surround the Nullarbor Plain which stretches across the land, and preserve the rugged coastline of the Great Australian Bight.

Because of its low rainfall, much of this country could be classed as desert. However, it is home to unique animals, and to a fascinating range of plants which survive the dry seasons in comfort then flower and seed in abundance once rain falls.

Opposite: Grass-trees, spinifex and a flat-topped hill, typical of aridland.

Nambung National Park

Nambung National Park, famous for its Pinnacles and Painted Desert, is an area of coastal dunes, heathlands and sandplains near the crayfishing town of Cervantes, 245 kilometres north of Perth.

The fantastic Pinnacles were formed many thousands of years ago, as rainwater seeped through the sand dunes and dissolved out lime. This cemented sand together to form pillars and columns, which were later exposed as the dunes were shifted by the sea wind.

Opposite and right: The Pinnacles, Nambung National Park.

69

Kalbarri National Park

Above: Kalbarri National Park offers spectacular scenes for the photographer.

Kalbarri National Park, around 530 kilometres north of Perth, is noted for its scenic splendours, its wildflowers, which blossom from August into early summer, and its wildlife. The multicoloured rock for which the area is famous, the Tumblegooda Sandstone, was laid down under the sea around 400 million years ago. When upheavals within the earth raised the sea bed, the Murchison River, with wind-blown sand and rain, carved the rocks into gorges, cliffs, ledges and lookouts.

Opposite: Nature's Window, Kalbarri National Park.
Following pages: Zuytdorp Cliffs rise up to 170 metres above the Indian Ocean between Kalbarri and Steep Point, Shark Bay.

Monkey Mia, Peron Peninsula.

Monkey Mia

A Bottlenose Dolphin invites contact with humans.

François Peron National Park is named after a naturalist who visited the area on *Le Géographe* in 1801 and 1803. The park occupies much of the Peron Peninsula which juts into the Indian Ocean 400 kilometres north of the port of Geraldton, and helps enclose the waters of Shark Bay.

A pod of around 300 Bottlenose Dolphins feed on fish and other marine life in the bay. A number of these dolphins regularly come to the shallow waters off Monkey Mia, 26 kilometres from the town of Denham, to interact with humans. These dolphins are not trained, rather, they have chosen to participate of their own free will. For the dolphins' protection, feeding is supervised by the local park rangers.

Shark Bay

Above: Water evaporates from Shark Bay's lagoons, leaving crusts of salt crystals.   *Opposite:* The soil of the Peron Peninsula is a dramatic red in colour.

Shark Bay is a World Heritage Area, protecting examples of the world's oldest surviving lifeform, the mounds of blue-green algae called stromatolites, which live in Hamelin Pool.

A number of rare and endangered animals live in the area, both on land and in the waters of Shark Bay. In the bay, vast banks of seagrass sustain groups of Dugongs, shy sea mammals which shun human attention.

Following pages: Kennedy Range National Park, 160 kilmetres east of Carnarvon.

The Gascoyne River

The Gascoyne River flows to the Indian Ocean at Carnarvon through some of Australia's driest country. Its steep red banks are lined with tall eucalypts and where billabongs have been cut off by the river breaking through a bend, the still waters attract birds of all kinds, kangaroos, emus and other creatures.

Gascoyne Junction, where the Lyons River joins the Gascoyne, is 177 kilometres east of Carnarvon. The adventurous traveller will journey another 315 kilometres and experience the stunning sight of Mt Augustus, the world's greatest rock.

Waterhole at Gascoyne Junction. The massive trees provide nesting sites for parrots and many other birds.

Mt Augustus National Park

Mt Augustus, the biggest rock in the world, stands in its own National Park.

Although Mt Augustus, 492 kilometres from Carnarvon, rises 1106 metres above sea level and is twice the size of Uluṟu, it appears far less spectacular because of its stepped formation and the sparse vegetation growing on its flanks. Its core is granite, estimated to be around 1750 million years old. To the Aboriginal people of the area, this immense rock represented the body of a traveller called Burringurrah, speared as he travelled through the area.

Karijini National Park

Karijini National Park, in the Pilbara of north-western Western Australia, is the State's second largest national park. Its landscapes are dominated by iron-ore-rich rock which forms one of the State's most notable natural resources, and gives the country its distinctive red colour. This magnificent area is brutally hot in summer, but its ranges, gorges, wildlife and wildflowers make visiting it a compelling experience. A visit between May and August will find warm, sunny days and crisp, clear nights, perfect weather for the exploration of landmarks such as Dales Gorge, Joffre Falls, Weano Gorge and Mt Bruce, Western Australia's second highest peak.

A distant view of the Hamersley Range, Karijini National Park.

Hamersley Range

Few living things can survive without water. Australia's aridland plants and animals are adapted to going for long periods on a minimum of moisture, but a waterhole such as that shown here, nestled in a gorge in the Hamersley Range, becomes a focus for wildlife. At noon, such an oasis is quiet and still. Visit just before dawn, or sit quietly on a fallen log for an hour or so before and after sunset, and you will be amazed at the number of creatures which warily make their way to the water to drink.

Left: Waterhole in a gorge in the Hamersley Range.
Following pages: Landscape with clumps of spinifex and Ghost Gums, Karijini National Park.

Gorge wall, pool and waterfall, Karijini National Park.

Weano Gorge, Karijini National Park.

The Pilbara

The rocks of the Hamersley Range were laid down on the sea floor 2500 million years ago. Today, this ancient stone has been carved by seasonal streams into spectacular gorges such as Weano, Dales and Hancock. Many can be appreciated fully only by energetic climbing, or by exploring at water level. The deepest, permanent pools harbour aquatic creatures of all kinds. The Aboriginal word for this region, "Pilbara", means "freshwater fish", which pays tribute to the inhabitants of these remarkable bodies of water.

Marble Bar

Gold was discovered near the town of Marble Bar in 1890 and thousands flocked to search for the precious metal.

Today the town, which takes its name from the impressive ribboned bar of jasper on the Coongan River, 5 kilometres away, is connected with tin and manganese mining. Marble Bar in summertime has the reputation of being the hottest place on Earth. In winter, the weather is delightful and a visit to the famous "marble bar" is a memorable experience.

Banded jasper gives Marble Bar its name.

Broome

Above: Luggers stranded at low tide, Broome.

North of Eighty Mile Beach, at the southern edge of the Kimberley, lies Broome. From this port, luggers carried divers who harvested oysters for their mother-of-pearl shells and, they hoped, fabulous pearls. Today, the world wears cultivated pearls, plastics have replaced pearl buttons, and divers are spared the perils of the sea. Broome's multicultural population, a legacy of the pearling days, together with its historic interest and the beauty of its setting, make the town a rewarding stopover on any journey of exploration. Cable Beach and Gantheaume Point are of particular interest.

Opposite: The rocks of Gantheaume Point, near Broome.

94

Moving the mob across a Kimberley plain, past a pair of Boab trees which, in winter, are devoid of leaves.

The Kimberley

The Kimberley is tropical monsoon country, where a warm dry winter sees trees drop their leaves and grasses brown off. With summer's bountiful tropical downpours, the land renews itself and cattle grow fat. Wildlife multiplies and rivers and billabongs are alive with birds – and crocodiles.

This is one of the world's final frontiers, a land of vast spaces, rugged ranges and wilderness, often inaccessible by road, and best visited in the cooler months of the year. In the Kimberley, there are still discoveries to be made and adventures to be lived.

Wilderness unparalleled

A stunning landscape in the Prince Regent Nature Reserve.

The Prince Regent River and its surrounding territory, in the
north of the Kimberley, is an area of magnificent wilderness,
classified as a World Biosphere Reserve.

The tide rises and falls around 11 metres in Walcott Inlet.

Walcott Inlet, a drowned river valley, extends about 30 kilometres inland from Collier Bay. No roads penetrate this wild area, one of the world's most awe-inspiring landscapes.

Bell Creek Reserve

The Kimberley is a vast area, which includes landscapes as diverse as rugged ranges, flat-topped hills termed "jump-ups", wide grassy plains, and isolated rainforest remnants, in which live unique species of plants and animals. In the cooler dry season, it is comparatively easy to explore much of the Kimberley, except for the north-east, by vehicle. In the Wet, when monsoons bring frequent, torrential rain, unsealed roads become impassable. This is a country which keeps its secrets close, but which repays alert travellers with vistas of scenic grandeur, and cameos of beauty which linger in the memory long after the difficulties of the journey undertaken to discover them are forgotten.

A place to cherish in Bell Creek Reserve.

Waterfall, Bell Creek Reserve.

Above: Boab trees on the floodplain of the Fitzroy River, near Derby, a major port for the West Kimberley.   *Following pages:* Windjana Gorge National Park.

A spiritual heritage

Aboriginal people have lived in the Kimberley for many tens of thousands of years. Their relationship with the land, and the spiritual and cultural heritage arising from this interaction, are reflected in their traditional rock art. This art was not created for entertainment and, if discovered, should be left exactly as it was when first sighted.

Opposite: Aboriginal artwork is sheltered by this rock's overhang.

Kimberley landscapes

A billabong on the Bernet River.

A river winds across a plain in a series of S bends. Eventually it cuts through the middle section of the S, isolating a small, curved lake called a billabong. Kimberley billabongs are places to see waterbirds, waterlilies, kangaroos, fish — and crocodiles. The fish-eating Freshwater Crocodile is harmless to large animals unless provoked, but watch out for the larger broad-snouted, possibly man-eating Saltwater Crocodile.

Above: Rock formations in Mirima National Park, near Kununurra.

Following pages: The Bungle Bungles, Purnululu National Park.

Around 350 million years ago, much of the Kimberley lay beneath a tropical sea. Sandstone was formed from sediment deposited on the floor of this sea: limestone is the remains of a primeval coral reef. Both are common in today's Kimberley. Formations like those shown above occur where a capping of harder rock protects the layered stone from weathering away at the same rate as the surrounding area.

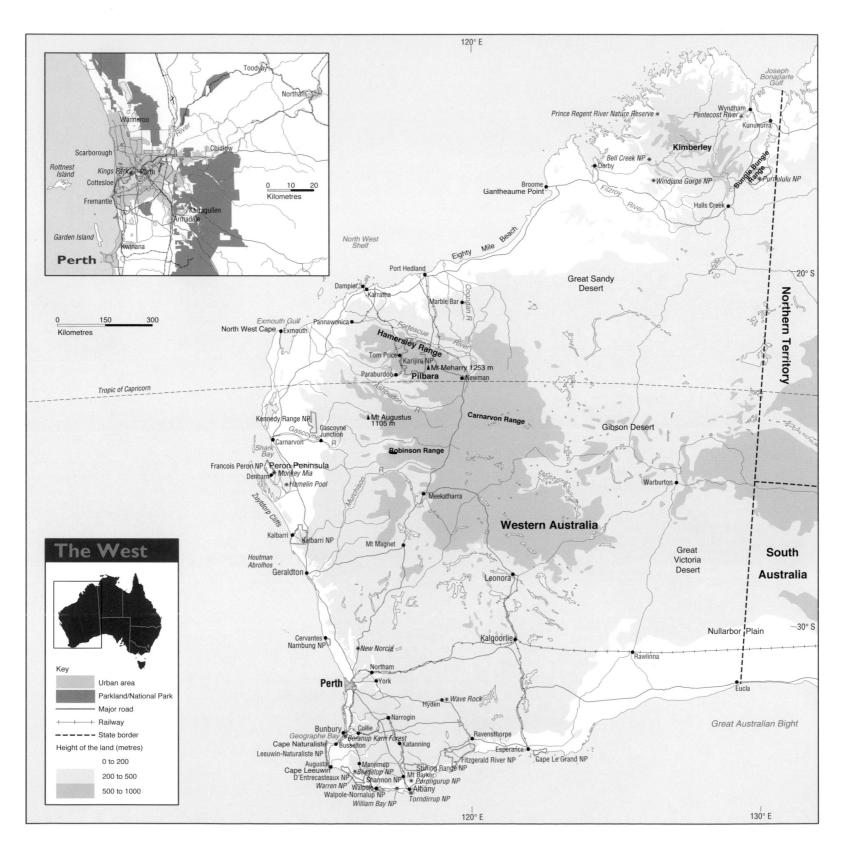

Perth

Toodyay
Northam
Warneroo
Scarborough
Chidlow
Swan River
Rottnest Island
Kings Park
Perth
Cottesloe
Fremantle
Karragullen
Armadale
Garden Island
Kwinana

0   10   20
Kilometres

The West

Key
Urban area
Parkland/National Park
Major road
Railway
State border
Height of the land (metres)
0 to 200
200 to 500
500 to 1000

0   150   300
Kilometres

Joseph Bonaparte Gulf
Prince Regent River Nature Reserve
Wyndham
Pentecost River
Kununurra
Kimberley
Bell Creek NP
Derby
Windjana Gorge NP
Bungle Bungle Range
Purnululu NP
Broome
Gantheaume Point
Halls Creek
Fitzroy River
Eighty Mile Beach
North West Shelf
Port Hedland
Great Sandy Desert
20° S
Dampier
Karratha
Marble Bar
Coongan R
Pannawonica
Exmouth Gulf
North West Cape
Exmouth
Fortescue River
Hamersley Range
Tom Price
Karijini NP
Mt Meharry 1253 m
Paraburdoo
Pilbara
Newman
Ashburton
Tropic of Capricorn
Kennedy Range NP
Mt Augustus 1105 m
Carnarvon Range
Gascoyne Junction
Gascoyne R
Carnarvon
Shark Bay
Robinson Range
Gibson Desert
Francois Peron NP
Peron Peninsula
Monkey Mia
Denham
Hamelin Pool
Murchison R
Meekatharra
Warburton
Zuytdorp Cliffs
Western Australia
Kalbarri
Kalbarri NP
Mt Magnet
Great Victoria Desert
South Australia
Houtman Abrolhos
Geraldton
Leonora
Cervantes
Nambung NP
Kalgoorlie
Nullarbor Plain
30° S
New Norcia
Rawlinna
Northam
York
Eucla
Perth
Hyden
Wave Rock
Narrogin
Great Australian Bight
Bunbury
Collie
Geographe Bay
Boranup Karri Forest
Cape Naturaliste
Busselton
Katanning
Ravensthorpe
Leeuwin-Naturaliste NP
Esperance
Cape Le Grand NP
Augusta
Manjimup
Fitzgerald River NP
Cape Leeuwin
Beedelup NP
Stirling Range NP
D'Entrecasteaux NP
Shannon NP
Mt Barker
Warren NP
Walpole
Porongurup NP
Walpole-Nornalup NP
Albany
William Bay NP
Torndirrup NP
Northern Territory
120° E
130° E

114

Wandering the West

At every turn of a Western Australian road, the traveller realises the magnificence of Australia's landscapes. Closer investigation highlights the unique relationships which have been established between plants and animals in this western part of the continent. It would take more than one lifetime to get to know Western Australia as it deserves. This third of the Australian continent keeps its secrets well, its fertile south-western corner separated from its tropical north by many kilometres of aridland. The coastal margin of Western Australia is now world-famous for its wildflowers, marine life and holiday atmosphere (witness the pilgrimages made to the springtime sandplains, to Monkey Mia and Rottnest Island). Now travellers are discovering the Pilbara, the Kimberley and the Goldfields. For the nature lover, the bushwalker, the photographer, or the adventurer, the West is a dream come true. Those who enjoy natural beauty, but who also savour the delights which civilisation has to offer, will find that warmth, friendliness and hospitality are all part of the Western Australian way of life.

Previous pages: Crossing the Pentecost River.

Steve Parish

World-famous photographer Steve Parish began his remarkable career by recording marine life off Australia's coasts. After discovering the fascinations to be found in the rainforest and its wild creatures, he has spent much of his life journeying Australia to photograph its landscapes, plants, animals and people. He then extended his range of subjects to capture on film the character of Australia's cities and towns.

The magnificent library of images that has resulted has become the heart of Steve Parish Publishing Pty Ltd. Through the firm's publications, Steve is realising his dream of sharing Australia with the world.

Western Australia is one in a collection of titles that present the incomparable beauty of the southern continent in superb photographs and text. As Steve comments: "After a lifetime of travel and asking questions, I have only just begun to discover how much there is to learn about Australia. I hope these books arouse in others a desire like mine to explore and to appreciate this wonderful country."

Index

First published by Steve Parish Publishing Pty Ltd
PO Box 1058, Archerfield, Queensland 4108, Australia

© copyright Steve Parish Publishing Pty Ltd

ISBN 1 74021041 7

Photography: Steve Parish
Text: Pat Slater, SPP Australia

Map supplied by MAPgraphics
Printed in Singapore
Cover design: Leanne Staff, SPP Australia

**Designed, edited and produced at the
Steve Parish Publishing Studios, Australia**

www.steveparish.com.au